A MACDONALD CHILDREN'S BOOK

First Published in Great Britain by
Macdonald Children's Books
Simon & Schuster International Group
Wolsey House, Wolsey Road
Hemel Hempstead HP2 5SS

Printed in Belgium by
Proost International Book Production

BRITISH LIBRARY CATALOGUING IN PUBLICATION DATA

Anderson, David, *1952–*
Mutiny on the Bounty
1. Great Britain. Royal Navy. Sailing
vessels: Bounty (ship). Mutiny
I. Title II. Lincoln, Margarette
III. National Maritime Museum
359.1'334

ISBN 0-356-16898-0
ISBN 0-356-16899-9 Pbk

Set in Caslon Old Face by Goodfellow & Egan

Editor: David Riley
Designer: Danuta Trebus
Production: Rosemary Bishop

Illustrators:
Paul Cooper: 11, 15, 18, 27, 31
Mike Embden: 10, 16–17, 28(T)
Brian Sweet: 6–7, 8–9, 19, 20–1, 26–7, 28–9(B), 30–1(T), 32–3, 36–7, 38–9, 40

Photographs:
National Maritime Museum: 3, 9, 10, 12, 13, 15, 22, 23, 24–5, 29, 34, 35, 41(L), 42(T), 43
Private Collection: 8, 14(T), 39, 41(R), 42(L)
Mary Evans Picture Library: 35
Bridgeman Art Library: Back cover
British Film Institute Films Collection: 42(B)

Dedication
For Rosemary, Isobel and Desmond

Acknowledgements
The authors would like to thank the following members of staff at the National Maritime Museum for their help and advice:
Robert Baldwin, Pat Blackett Barber, Peter Ince, Dr Eric Kentley, Hélène Mitchell, Rina Prentice, Dr Stephen Riley and Barbara Tomlinson. Thanks are also due to the Photographic Department, particularly to Barry Cash, David Spence and Jim Stevenson; also to Margaret Hudson and Jane Wright for typing the text, and to all other Museum staff who contributed their help.

Finally, the authors wish to thank Josephine Anderson and Andrew Lincoln for their advice and support.

The editor would like to thank Fiona Macdonald for her help and advice.

Title page: William Bligh in Captain's uniform. In the background you can just see an outline of Tahiti and a Tahitian canoe.

THE MUTINY ON THE BOUNTY

DAVID ANDERSON
AND
MARGARETTE LINCOLN

Macdonald Children's Books

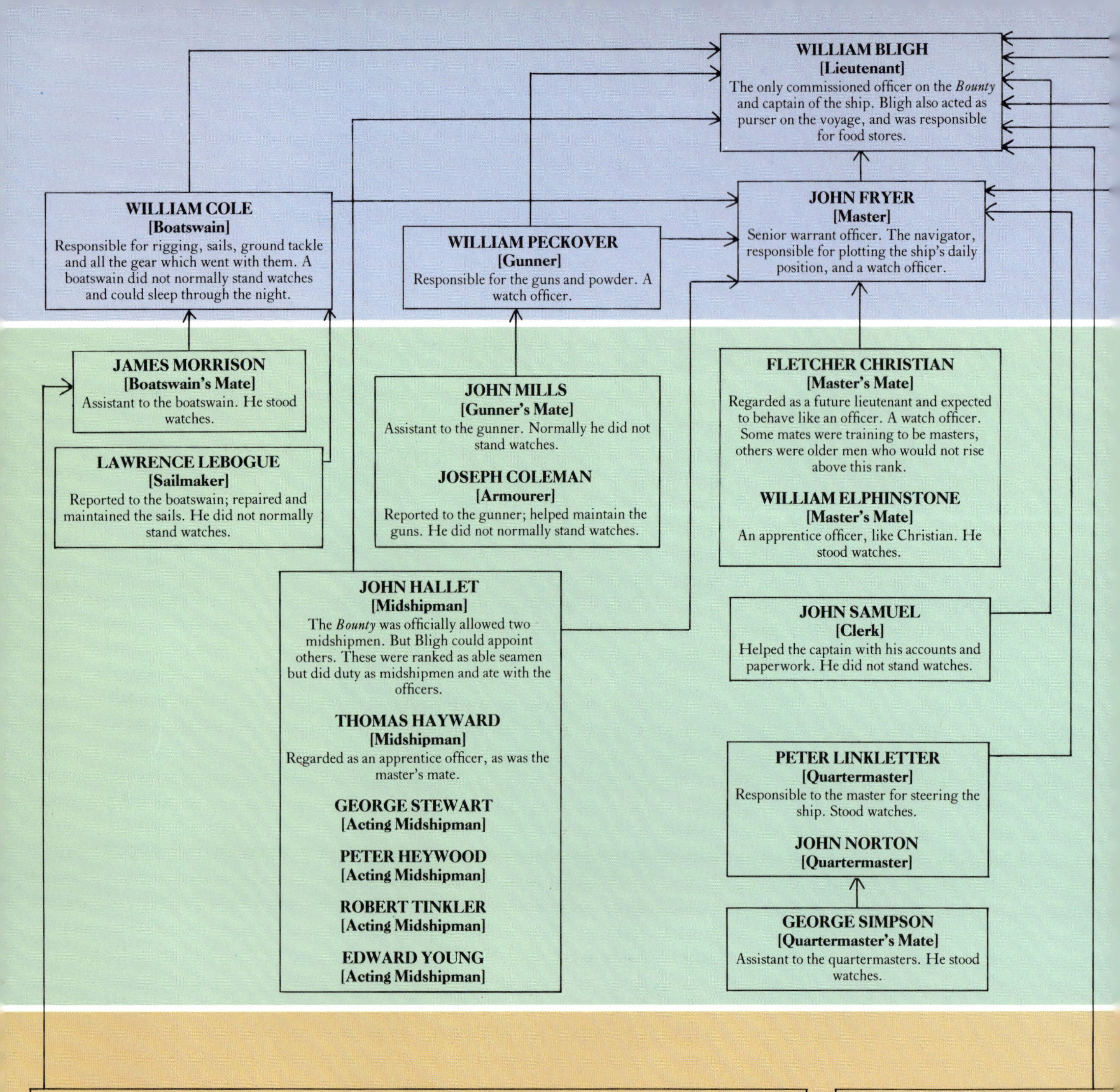

WILLIAM BLIGH
[Lieutenant]
The only commissioned officer on the Bounty and captain of the ship. Bligh also acted as purser on the voyage, and was responsible for food stores.
WILLIAM COLE
[Boatswain]
Responsible for rigging, sails, ground tackle and all the gear which went with them. A boatswain did not normally stand watches and could sleep through the night.
WILLIAM PECKOVER
[Gunner]
Responsible for the guns and powder. A watch officer.
JOHN FRYER
[Master]
Senior warrant officer. The navigator, responsible for plotting the ship's daily position, and a watch officer.
JAMES MORRISON
[Boatswain's Mate]
Assistant to the boatswain. He stood watches.
LAWRENCE LEBOGUE
[Sailmaker]
Reported to the boatswain; repaired and maintained the sails. He did not normally stand watches.
JOHN MILLS
[Gunner's Mate]
Assistant to the gunner. Normally he did not stand watches.
JOSEPH COLEMAN
[Armourer]
Reported to the gunner; helped maintain the guns. He did not normally stand watches.
FLETCHER CHRISTIAN
[Master's Mate]
Regarded as a future lieutenant and expected to behave like an officer. A watch officer. Some mates were training to be masters, others were older men who would not rise above this rank.
WILLIAM ELPHINSTONE
[Master's Mate]
An apprentice officer, like Christian. He stood watches.
JOHN HALLET
[Midshipman]
The Bounty was officially allowed two midshipmen. But Bligh could appoint others. These were ranked as able seamen but did duty as midshipmen and ate with the officers.
THOMAS HAYWARD
[Midshipman]
Regarded as an apprentice officer, as was the master's mate.
GEORGE STEWART
[Acting Midshipman]
PETER HEYWOOD
[Acting Midshipman]
ROBERT TINKLER
[Acting Midshipman]
EDWARD YOUNG
[Acting Midshipman]
JOHN SAMUEL
[Clerk]
Helped the captain with his accounts and paperwork. He did not stand watches.
PETER LINKLETTER
[Quartermaster]
Responsible to the master for steering the ship. Stood watches.
JOHN NORTON
[Quartermaster]
GEORGE SIMPSON
[Quartermaster's Mate]
Assistant to the quartermasters. He stood watches.
THOMAS BURKITT
[Able Seaman]
Worked the ship, eg managed the sails, raised the anchors, worked the pumps, stood watches.
MICHAEL BYRNE
[Able Seaman and Musician]
Practically blind and therefore not able to do duty as an able seaman. He played the fiddle to entertain the crew and to accompany their dancing.
THOMAS ELLISON
[Able Seaman]
HENRY HILLBRANT
[Able Seaman and Cooper]
Responsible for maintaining the barrels in which provisions were stored.
ROBERT LAMB
[Able Seaman and Butcher]
Responsible for slaughtering the live animals carried on board for food, and preparing the carcasses.
ISAAC MARTIN
[Able Seaman]
WILLIAM McCOY
[Able Seaman]
JOHN MILLWARD
[Able Seaman]
WILLIAM MUSPRAT
[Able Seaman and Steward]
Servant to the officers, eg he waited on them at meal times.
MATTHEW QUINTAL
[Able Seaman]
RICHARD SKINNER
[Able Seaman]
ALEXANDER SMITH
[Able Seaman]
JOHN SUMNER
[Able Seaman]
MATTHEW THOMPSON
[Able Seaman]
JAMES VALENTINE
[Able Seaman]
JOHN WILLIAMS
[Able Seaman]
THOMAS HALL
[Able Seaman and Cook]
Responsible for cooking meals to be eaten by the crew. He reported directly to Bligh (in Bligh's role as purser) and did not stand watches.
JOHN SMITH
[Able Seaman and Commander's Cook]
Responsible for preparing food to be eaten at Bligh's table. He reported directly to Bligh (in Bligh's role as purser) and did not stand watches.

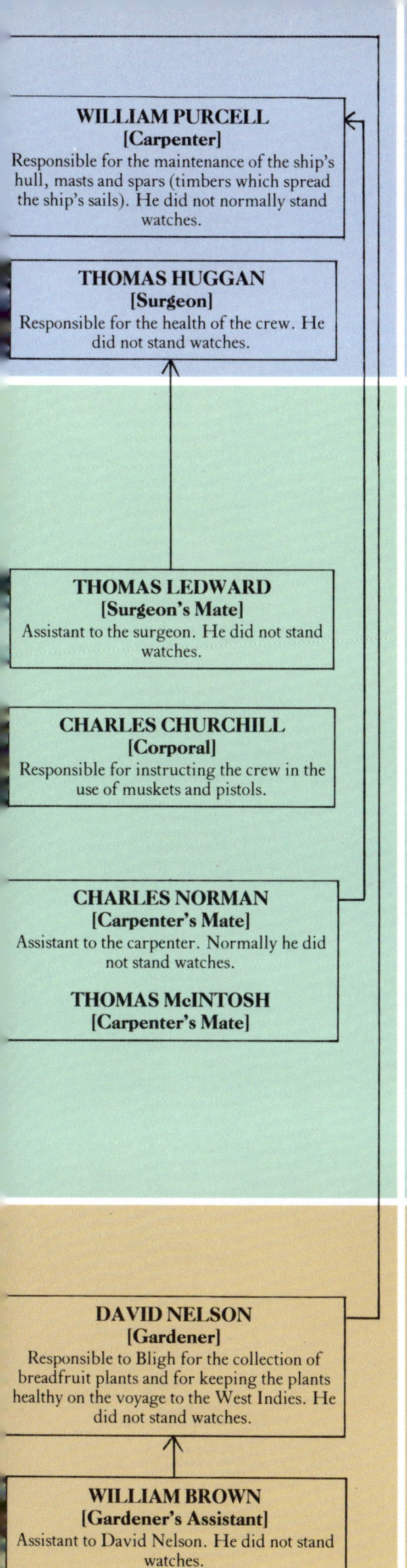
WILLIAM PURCELL
[Carpenter]
Responsible for the maintenance of the ship's hull, masts and spars (timbers which spread the ship's sails). He did not normally stand watches.
THOMAS HUGGAN
[Surgeon]
Responsible for the health of the crew. He did not stand watches.
THOMAS LEDWARD
[Surgeon's Mate]
Assistant to the surgeon. He did not stand watches.
CHARLES CHURCHILL
[Corporal]
Responsible for instructing the crew in the use of muskets and pistols.
CHARLES NORMAN
[Carpenter's Mate]
Assistant to the carpenter. Normally he did not stand watches.
THOMAS McINTOSH
[Carpenter's Mate]
DAVID NELSON
[Gardener]
Responsible to Bligh for the collection of breadfruit plants and for keeping the plants healthy on the voyage to the West Indies. He did not stand watches.
WILLIAM BROWN
[Gardener's Assistant]
Assistant to David Nelson. He did not stand watches.
WARRANT OFFICERS
[Specialists and craftsmen responsible directly to Bligh.]
INFERIOR OFFICERS
THE RATINGS, OR PEOPLE
[Responsible to Bligh but subject also to the discipline of other officers, chiefly the boatswain and his mate.]

Contents

The Mutiny

IT was 5.15 am on 28 April 1789. The *Bounty* was sailing peacefully across a calm, tropical sea. In his cabin,Captain Bligh sighed gently in his sleep. He felt certain that this voyage to the **South Seas** was going to be a great success. There had been a little trouble with the crew in Tahiti, perhaps, but that was behind them now. They were heading for the West Indies with a cargo of precious tropical trees; after that they would be homeward bound!

The captain's pleasant dreams were soon abruptly shattered. Suddenly, the door was flung open and four armed men burst into the room. They seized the captain roughly, and dragged him out of his bunk. He staggered and fell, but they hauled him to his feet. 'What is the meaning of this violence?' he demanded furiously. 'Hold your tongue, sir,' snapped Fletcher Christian, the second in command. Other members of the crew were crowding outside the cabin door, shouting and cursing. 'What's the matter?' Bligh asked, realising that he was in great danger. 'What's the matter?' In vain he tried to rouse the crew. 'Murder! Murder!' he cried. No one came to help him. Instead, his hands were tied behind his back and he was dragged, still in his shirt and nightcap, up the ladder and onto the deck.

There, a scene of total confusion met the captain's eyes. Instead of men working swiftly and efficiently at their early morning duties on board ship, he was confronted by mutineers, jeering noisily and brandishing their stolen weapons. Those members of the crew who had not joined in the mutiny stayed well out of the way, for fear of what might happen next. Fletcher Christian dragged Bligh over towards the mizzen mast, while a guard of mutineers surrounded him, aiming their **muskets** at his head. Even though he was in great danger, and terribly afraid, Bligh refused to give in. Defiantly, he glared at the mutineers and their guns. 'I dare you to fire at me!' he shouted.

It was almost unheard of for men to disobey officers and take control of a ship at sea. Unsure of their position, most waited uneasily on the turn of events. But at last, Mr Fryer, the master of the ship, persuaded the mutineers to let him up on deck. He hurried across to Fletcher Christian. 'Mr Christian,' he pleaded, 'consider what you are about!' Christian turned on him angrily. 'Hold your tongue, sir! Not another word, or you are a dead man!' Captain Bligh was trapped, a prisoner on board his own ship.

Young Bligh

William Bligh when he was a young midshipman.

WILLIAM Bligh was 34 years old in 1789, the time of the mutiny on the *Bounty*. He had spent half his life at sea. His father had been a customs officer in the busy port of Plymouth. He decided that young William should make **seafaring** his career. He knew that William would have to rely on hard work and a quick brain to win promotion, and so he made sure that he received a good education. At school, William was particularly good at maths. This early training helped him to become an expert navigator while he was still a young man.

Bligh's first job on board ship was as an able seaman, when he was just 16. He worked well, and continued to study **navigation.** News of this clever young sailor reached Captain Cook, the famous explorer, and, in 1776, when Bligh was only 21, he chose him as master of his ship *Resolution*. Bligh's job would be to make surveys and to draw up detailed **charts** of creeks and harbours, to help future navigators. He would be Cook's right-hand man.

Captain Cook and his crew set sail on a dangerous and exciting voyage of discovery. They landed on the Hawaiian Islands in the north Pacific, which were then unknown to European travellers. At first, the local people welcomed them, but soon the sailors had eaten more food than the natives could spare. There were quarrels, too, after local people stole various items from the sailors.

Captain Cook had a fiery temper. He was very angry about these thefts and decided to teach the islanders a lesson. He planned to capture one of the local chiefs and to hold him as a hostage until the stolen goods were returned. But this rather foolhardy plan went wrong. Cook and his raiding party were soon faced by an angry

crowd, and hopelessly outnumbered. The local people started throwing stones, and Cook was hit. He fired back, and, in panic, the local people began to attack the Europeans. Faced by the hostile mob, Cook's bodyguard of **marines** fired one round from their muskets and then fled. Captain Cook was clubbed down, and stabbed to death.

Bligh was shocked by Cook's murder. He had learned a lot from the great explorer during the voyage to Hawaii. On long voyages, sailors generally suffered from illness such as scurvy, caused by poor diet. To combat this, Cook insisted that his men eat wholesome food, even if they didn't like it. He stocked his ships with pickled cabbage and other foods containing essential vitamins to keep the crew healthy. Cook could be bad-tempered and shout and swear at his men, but they tolerated this, because they understood that he cared for them. Later, when Bligh took command of his own ship, he found out just how difficult it was to be as good a captain as Cook had been.

A portrait of Captain Cook, in his mid-forties.

The death of Captain Cook on a beach in Hawaii. The marines who should have protected him are retreating in one of the ship's boats.

Exploration and Trade

The *Bounty's* chronometer. In Bligh's time, chronometers were still extremely expensive, and not all captains owned one.

AFTER Cook's death, Bligh played an important part in navigating the *Resolution* home. He did this brilliantly, but no one acknowledged his achievement, and he was bitterly disappointed.

As Bligh left the *Resolution* for the last time, he stared around him at the huge number of ships in the mouth of the River Thames. This was the busiest stretch of water in the whole of Britain. A constant flow of merchant ships entered the Thames on their way to London, and others headed out to sea with cargoes bound for distant lands.

In Bligh's time, seafaring was a dangerous way to make a living. Voyages could often take many months, and ships quite often disappeared without trace. One problem was that sailors found it difficult to **fix their position** at sea. Navigation was becoming more scientific, but charts were often inaccurate and many ships were lost on uncharted rocks. Great skill was needed to avoid missing one's destination, or at worst, shipwreck.

No one understood this better than Bligh. He was an expert navigator, but he was using tools that were basic by today's standards. Then, as today, sailors used a **compass** to find the direction in which they were sailing. But even the best chart couldn't help if the captain didn't know exactly where he was! In order to discover this, sailors needed to know two things. One was their latitude – that is how far

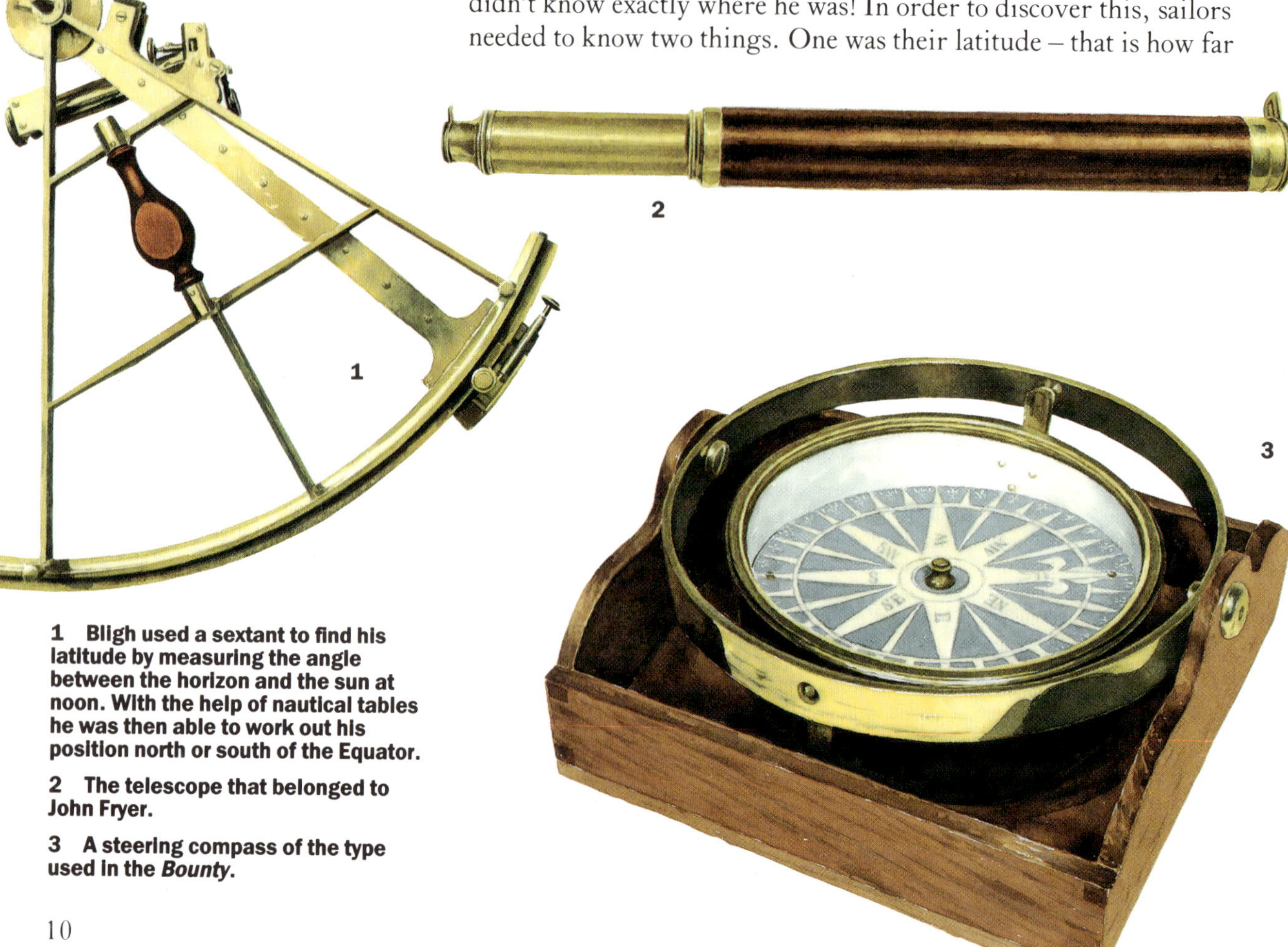

1 Bligh used a sextant to find his latitude by measuring the angle between the horizon and the sun at noon. With the help of nautical tables he was then able to work out his position north or south of the Equator.

2 The telescope that belonged to John Fryer.

3 A steering compass of the type used in the *Bounty*.

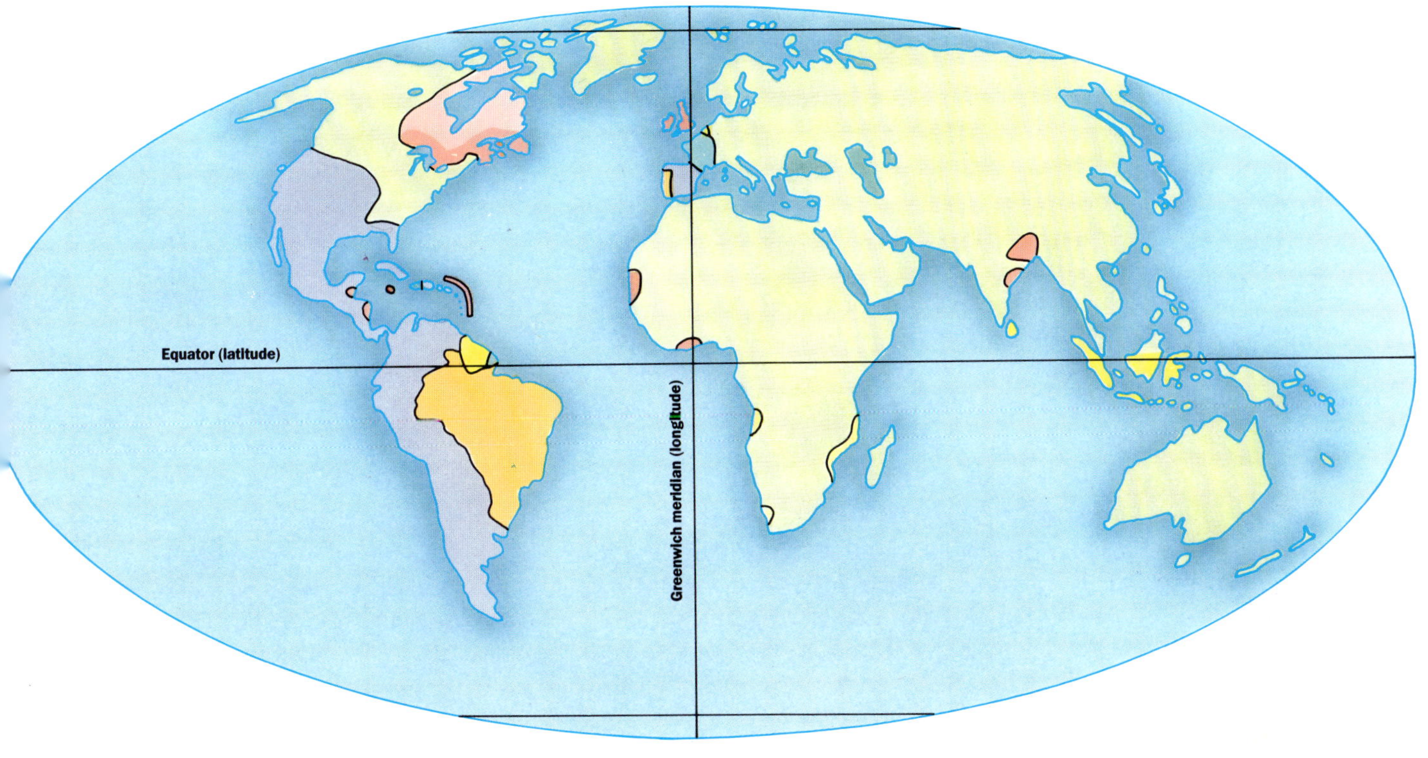

north or south they were (of an imaginary line, the Equator, which passes around the Earth at its widest point). The other was their longitude – that is how far east or west they were (of another imaginary line which passes through Greenwich, near London).

To find the ship's latitude, Bligh would have used a **sextant**, but the sky had to be clear so that he could take readings from the stars or the sun. If the sky was overcast, precise readings were impossible.

For centuries, sailors had no accurate way of working out their longitude, which can be measured by recording the difference of time between two places. But in 1761, Harrison perfected his chronometer, an extremely accurate clock, able to keep good time at sea. From then on, it was much easier to find out a ship's longitude. This made an enormous difference to trade. Sailing was still extremely hazardous, but captains could now take the shortest route between any two places, if the winds permitted.

Several European nations had earlier sent trading expeditions to establish **colonies** in distant parts of the world. The Portuguese, Spanish and Dutch had made huge profits in the Far East. Since navigators could now plot an exact route at sea, merchants realised that a country with accurate charts stood to make great wealth from trade. Bligh knew that this was the motive behind voyages of exploration, like Cook's, that aimed to chart the oceans as well as find new land. Cook had discovered many islands, but his discoveries hadn't been profitable. The government was anxious to change this situation.

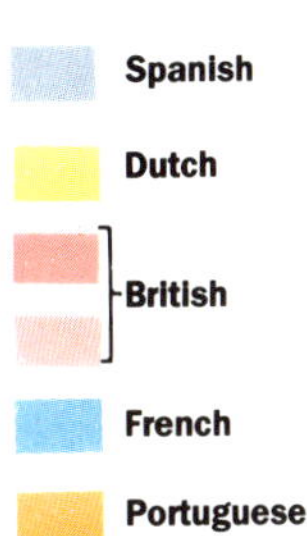

A map of the world in 1789, showing the colonies belonging to the different European nations. The lines of longitude and latitude are marked on the map.

Life in the Navy

In the eighteenth century, Britain had the best navy in the world. But many people today believe that its ships were like floating prisons, and that its sailors were miserable half-starved scum, who stumbled over the decks sodden with drink and reeling from the blows of the **lash**. This cannot be true. No successful navy could be run in this way.

Many sailors joined the navy when they were children. The largest ships had 50 or more boys aged from six to eighteen years, and employed a schoolmaster to teach them. At first the youngest boys found life on board ship frightening. Sailors used so many strange words that it seemed as if they spoke a different language. Everyone on board was divided into two **watches**. They ate, slept and worked in turn, depending on their watch. 'Nor could I think what world I was in', one sailor remembered, 'whether among spirits or devils. I thought myself always asleep or in a dream and never properly awake'.

As they grew older, the boys learned to make themselves useful; they carried gunpowder for the cannons from the powder room to the gun deck. Boys from poor families trained to become able seamen, or learned a trade by working with craftsmen like the ship's carpenter or the sailmaker. Wealthy families sent their sons to be servants to the captain or one of the other officers; when they grew up, they often became captains or lieutenants themselves.

Every activity on board ship, from hoisting the sails to hauling in the anchor, needed men who were strong and healthy. The navy realised that their crews must have plenty of good food every day if

Ship's biscuit, also called 'bread'. Biscuit was made from flour and water. It was carefully baked and packed in bags. The arrow mark showed that the biscuit was issued by the navy.

Ship's Rations

Each man on board ship was allowed generous rations each week:

3 kilograms bread/ship's biscuit
1.8 kilograms salted beef
900 grams salted pork
1.1 litres dried peas (usually cooked into mushy peas pudding)
1.7 litres oatmeal (for porridge or oatflakes)
170 grams butter or oil
240 grams cheese
32 litres beer

At times, there were extra rations of suet, raisins, vinegar and dried fish. The navy took care to buy good quality provisions, and to pack them carefully to last during long voyages. Salted meat, and dried ship's biscuit and peas could be kept for up to two years without going bad.

Sailors drinking on board ship. Heavy drinking was tolerated when the ship was in port, but at sea any sailor who was too drunk to do his work would be flogged.

A flogging, illustrated by George Cruikshank. Bligh did not have a reputation as a 'flogger' and was more lenient than other captains of his day.

they were going to do their jobs properly. But the basic navy rations did not provide them with all they needed to keep them healthy. They often went short of vitamin C, which is found in fresh fruit and vegetables. Without this vitamin, the sailors would fall ill with scurvy; their skins would become dry and scaly, their lips would crack, their gums would bleed and go rotten, and their teeth would fall out. By the late eighteenth century, the navy had discovered that sauerkraut (pickled cabbage) was a good source of vitamin C. It also kept well on long voyages. Although the sailors did not like it, it became part of their diet while at sea.

Life on board ship was uncomfortable and dangerous. Deaths were common. Sailors might drown in a shipwreck, or fall from the top of the masts, or suffocate if foul air escaped from the bilges at the bottom of a ship. They might be attacked by pirates or by an enemy warship. About half the sailors who signed on to join the navy died before the end of their period of service.

The men who faced all these risks had to be tough and able to think for themselves. Usually, sailors worked well together, not because of the threat of the lash, but because they knew that their safety depended upon it. There was also a tradition in the navy that sailors had a right to complain if they thought they were being unfairly treated. Most complaints were about pay, with a few about brutal captains. Occasionally, the sailors rioted in port, or refused to set sail. If their complaints were justified, and if no violence was used, then the sailors were not punished. But a mutiny at sea was rarer and a much more serious matter. It could endanger the whole ship, and the lives of everyone on board. The punishment for mutiny was death.

The quarterdeck of a merchant ship sailing home from the West Indies in 1775. Note the live animals carried for food.

Breadfruit Mission

Mrs Bligh at her marriage. Although she was not beautiful she was lively and good-humoured. She loyally supported Bligh in times of difficulty.

ONCE the crew of the *Resolution* had been **paid off**, Bligh was free to return to Plymouth. But his homecoming was not as joyful as he hoped it would be. His father had changed greatly in the four years Bligh had been away, and within two months he died. As his mother was already dead, Bligh reflected sadly that he had nothing now to hold him in Plymouth.

However, before long, he had happier things to think about. In 1775 he had met a girl called Elizabeth Betham. They had fallen in love, and she had promised to marry him when he returned from his voyage to the Pacific. Now he hurried to meet her, and they were married in 1781. Elizabeth's relations were rich and powerful; they would do what they could to help Bligh in his career. One of Elizabeth's uncles, Duncan Campbell, was a merchant, who shipped cargoes of sugar and rum from the plantations in the West Indies to England. He owned a fleet of ships, and, in 1783, he made Bligh master of one of them.

At this time, the owners of the sugar plantations were facing financial difficulties. It was always expensive to feed their slaves, because most food had to be shipped to the West Indies from America. Now costs were even higher, because war with America disrupted food supplies, and made shipping dangerous. The sugar merchants and plantation owners decided that they must search for a food crop that would grow well in the West Indies, and end the need to import supplies.

We don't know exactly what the outside of the *Bounty* looked like – only the ship's plans have survived. This is an impression of the *Bounty* in full sail by a modern artist, G Robinson.

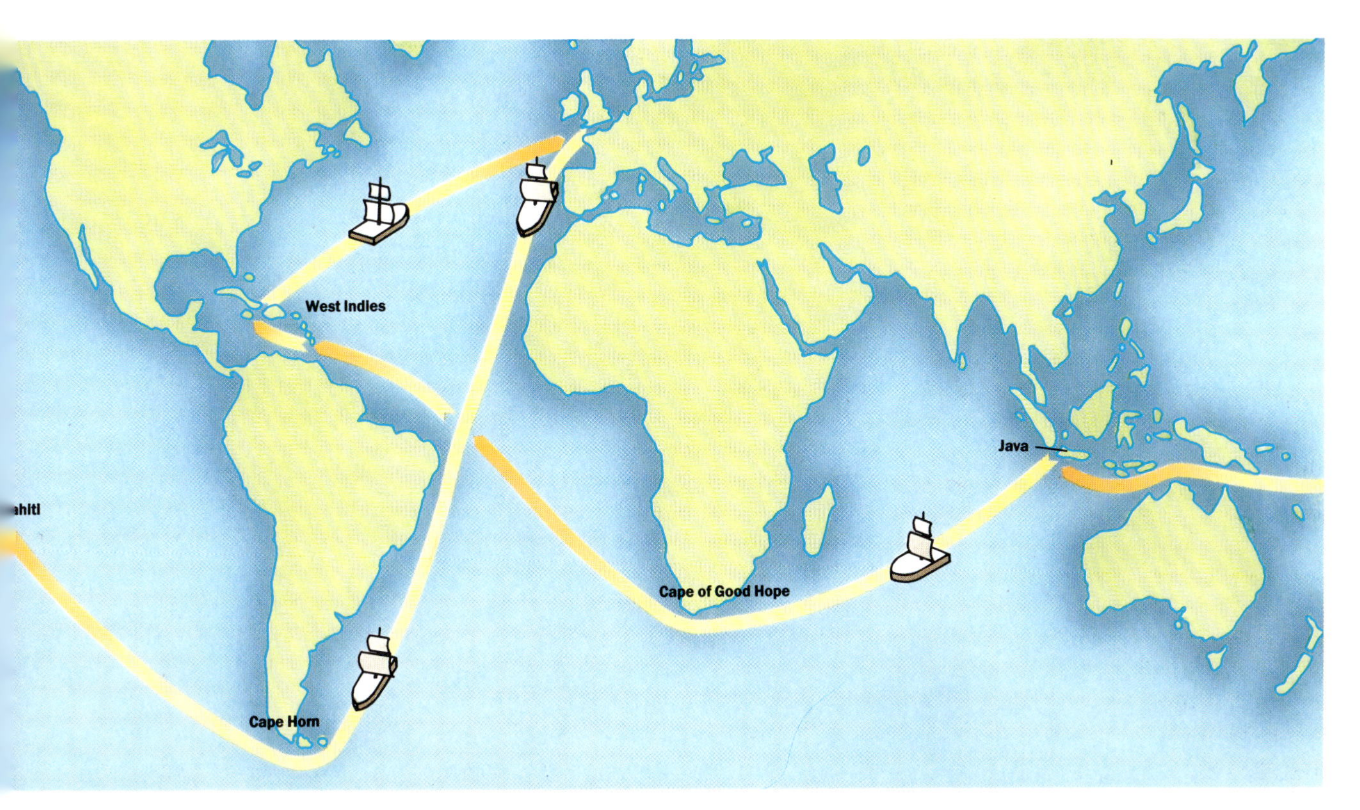

A map showing the shorter route to Tahiti, around Cape Horn. This was the route Bligh planned to take before storms drove him back.

In 1775, the Society for West Indian Merchants offered to pay the cost of importing a new food plant. And a scientific society, the Society of Arts, Manufactures and Commerce, promised a gold medal to anyone who could successfully transport six healthy, growing plants. Both societies thought that the breadfruit, which flourished in the islands of the Pacific Ocean, would be the most suitable species to introduce. This is how one explorer, William Dampier, described it, in 1688:

The breadfruit (as we call it) grows on a large tree, as big and high as our apple trees . . . The fruit grows on the boughs like apples; it is as big as a penny-loaf . . . of a round shape, and hath a thick tough rind. When the fruit is ripe it is yellow and soft, and the taste is sweet and pleasant. The natives gather it when full grown while it is green and hard; they then bake it in an oven, which scorcheth the rind and makes it black; but they scrape off the outside black crust and there remains a tender thin crust; and the inside is soft, tender and white like the crumb of a penny-loaf. There is neither seed nor stone in the inside, but all is of a pure substance, like bread . . .'

Bread growing on trees? It seemed too good to be true. No wonder the plantation owners were eager to bring the breadfruit tree to the West Indies. Sir Joseph Banks, President of the Royal Society, scientist and explorer, was enthusiastic about the breadfruit project, and in May 1787, plans were drawn up for a plant-collecting voyage. Bligh's skills as a navigator were becoming well known, and he was offered the command of this great expedition. It was the chance of a lifetime!

An engraving of breadfruit from Tahiti.

The *Bounty*

AS soon as Bligh knew that he had been given the command of the breadfruit mission, he hurried down to **Deptford** to inspect the *Bounty*, the ship he would be sailing in. It had been chosen for him by the **Admiralty** and by Sir Joseph Banks.

When Bligh first saw the *Bounty*, his heart sank. She was a little merchant ship, only 28 metres long. She was too small for such a long voyage, but there was no chance now of getting a bigger ship. Bligh felt even more worried when he went below decks. On the orders of Banks, the great cabin had been turned into a 'garden' for the breadfruit, complete with a complicated system of water pipes and drains. Banks was obviously more concerned about the plants than the comfort of the crew. Bligh knew how overcrowded the little vessel would seem.

The more Bligh learned about the Admiralty's arrangements for the voyage, the angrier he became. Because the *Bounty* was so small, there would be no room for marines on the ship, and no **commissioned officer** apart from himself. This meant that Bligh would have to maintain discipline all on his own. The Admiralty also refused to promote Bligh to the rank of captain. He would be in charge of the ship of course, and would be called captain by his men. But officially, he would have to command the *Bounty* as a mere lieutenant. Bligh complained bitterly that he was to be paid only £70 a year during the voyage, instead of the £500 a year he had been paid by Campbell. It was clear that the Admiralty cared little about this breadfruit expedition.

Bligh recruited 44 men to serve as crew on board the *Bounty*. They were typical of a ship's company 200 years ago – mainly in their 20s and unmarried. John Fryer, the ship's master, and Thomas Huggan, the surgeon, were the first men that Bligh recruited. Both came with good references, but Bligh soon discovered that the overweight Huggan

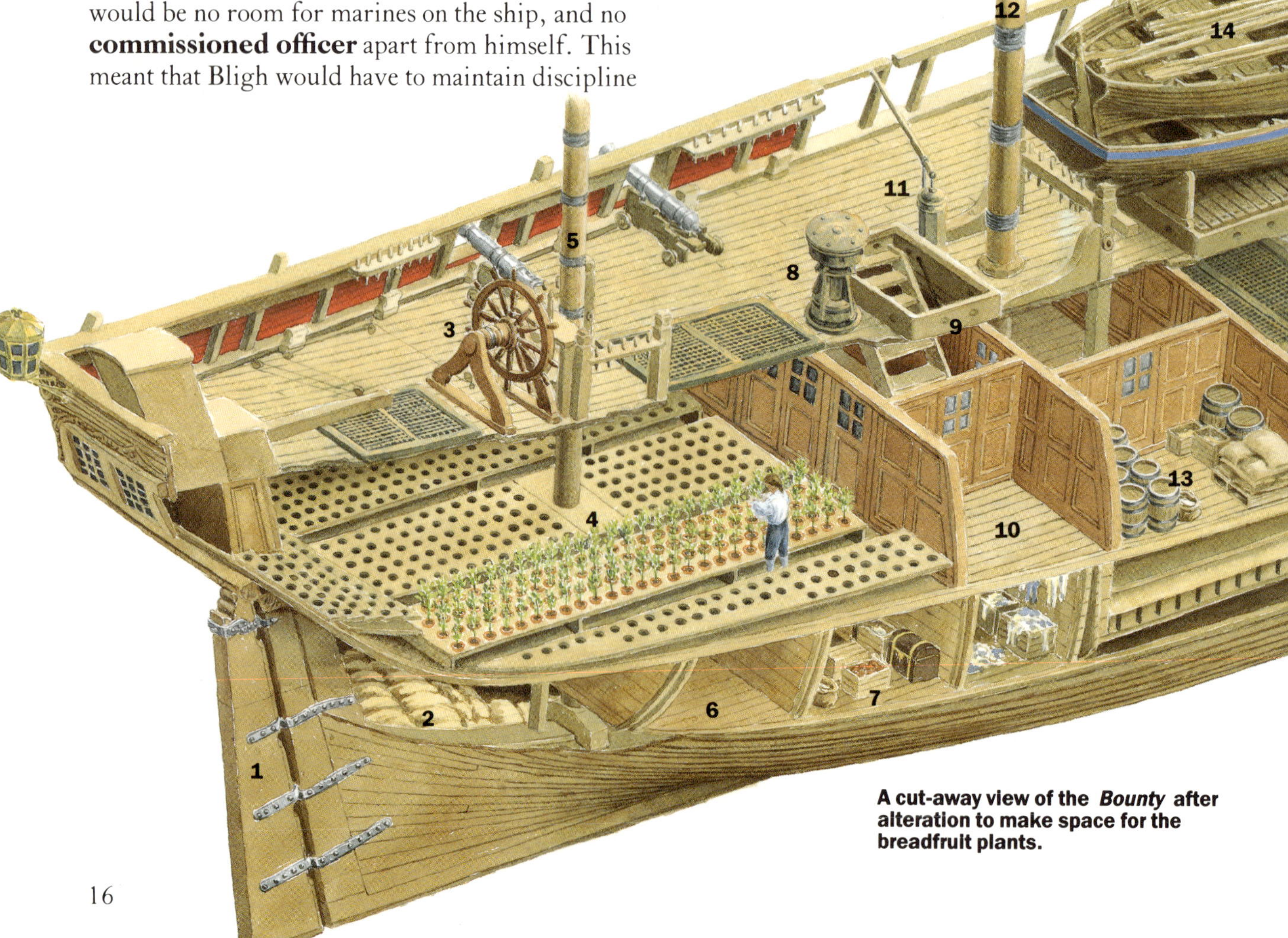

A cut-away view of the *Bounty* after alteration to make space for the breadfruit plants.

1 Rudder
2 Bread room
3 Ship's wheel
4 Great cabin (converted into a garden)
5 Mizzen mast
6 Gunner's cabin
7 Bligh's store-room. Here he kept his chest and a private supply of food and drink
8 Capstan (to raise and lower the anchor)
9 Hatchway
10 Bligh's cabin
11 Bilge pump
12 Main mast
13 Pantry (store-room for food)
14 Cutter and launch (a third boat – the jolly-boat – was towed behind the ship)
15 Hold
16 Living area for crew
17 Carpenter's cabin
18 Fore mast
19 Galley stove
20 Carpenter's store-room

THE staple food for the voyage was 'bread' – tough, dry ship's biscuits, which were usually riddled with live weevils. In addition, there were casks of salted beef and pork, sacks of dried peas, and barrels of rum, beer and wine. Bligh was determined to prevent his men getting scurvy, and took a large supply of sauerkraut and portable soup. Fresh meat was a special treat at sea and also helped to prevent scurvy. The *Bounty* carried a dozen hens, half a dozen sheep and some pigs, which lived together in four cages on the deck. There was also a dog, but this was, of course, a mascot and not for eating.

was a drunkard and tried to get rid of him. Just before the *Bounty* left England, Bligh added Thomas Ledward to the crew as surgeon's mate. The youngest crew members were Peter Heywood and John Hallett, aged 15. Bligh's wife, Elizabeth, had known their relatives for many years. Peter Heywood was the apple of his parents' eye, and they had great hopes of him from this voyage. Lawrence Lebogue, the sail-maker, and William Peckover, the gunner, had sailed with Bligh before. He knew they were both loyal men and gladly took them on.

Early in September, a strongly-made sailor of 22 joined the crew. Fletcher Christian was a clever young man who had sailed with Bligh twice before on his voyages to the West Indies. The two had become close friends. Bligh was a perfectionist, and was quick to criticise any sailor who failed to meet his own high standards. Christian described him as, 'a very passionate man' but, he added, 'I believe I have learnt how to handle him'. Christian himself was excitable, sometimes lively and cheerful, and sometimes sunk in black depression. Yet Bligh had great faith in his abilities and promoted him to master's mate when he joined the ship. No one could have foreseen how a quarrel between these two men would decide the fate of everyone else on board ship.

Raging Seas

BLIGH knew that the journey to Tahiti would not be easy. It was already September, dangerously late in the year. If he was delayed during the early stages of the journey, then the terrible winter storms off Cape Horn would force him to take a longer, eastwards, route round the Cape of Good Hope.

Although the *Bounty* was ready, delays with orders and bad weather meant that it wasn't until 23 December that the ship finally set sail. The great breadfruit expedition had begun!

Even then, things did not go smoothly. The ship was damaged by violent storms, and the sailors became tired and weak. Eventually, they anchored at Tenerife, for repairs and fresh supplies. Back at sea, Bligh gave the men a chance to recover their strength by organising a three-watch system (on duty for four hours out of every twelve, rather than the usual four hours in every eight). This gave the crew more rest, but it meant appointing an extra watch officer to supervise them. Bligh chose Christian, and a few weeks later promoted him to the rank of acting lieutenant. Fryer was particularly jealous, because Christian, a younger man, had been promoted over his head.

Despite the bad weather, Bligh was determined to attempt the shorter route to Tahiti, through the treacherous seas around Cape Horn. For three weeks he battled against wind and waves until the *Bounty* began to leak and the men fell ill. At last he had to admit defeat, and gave the order for the ship to turn round. Wearily, they sailed eastwards across the Atlantic, and on 22 May anchored at the Cape of Good Hope. Before them lay 6,000 **miles** of empty ocean. During this final stage of the voyage, isolated from the world, Bligh began to have trouble with his crew, who were quarrelsome after five months cooped up together on board ship. Now there were several challenges to his authority: the carpenter, Purcell, refused to obey orders, Fryer refused to sign the account books, and the surgeon was constantly drunk. The *Bounty* eventually reached Tahiti on 26 October 1788 after a voyage of 27,086 miles, in dangerous and difficult conditions. Bligh had succeeded in safely bringing his ship to its destination, but, by the end of the voyage, many of his men no longer respected him.

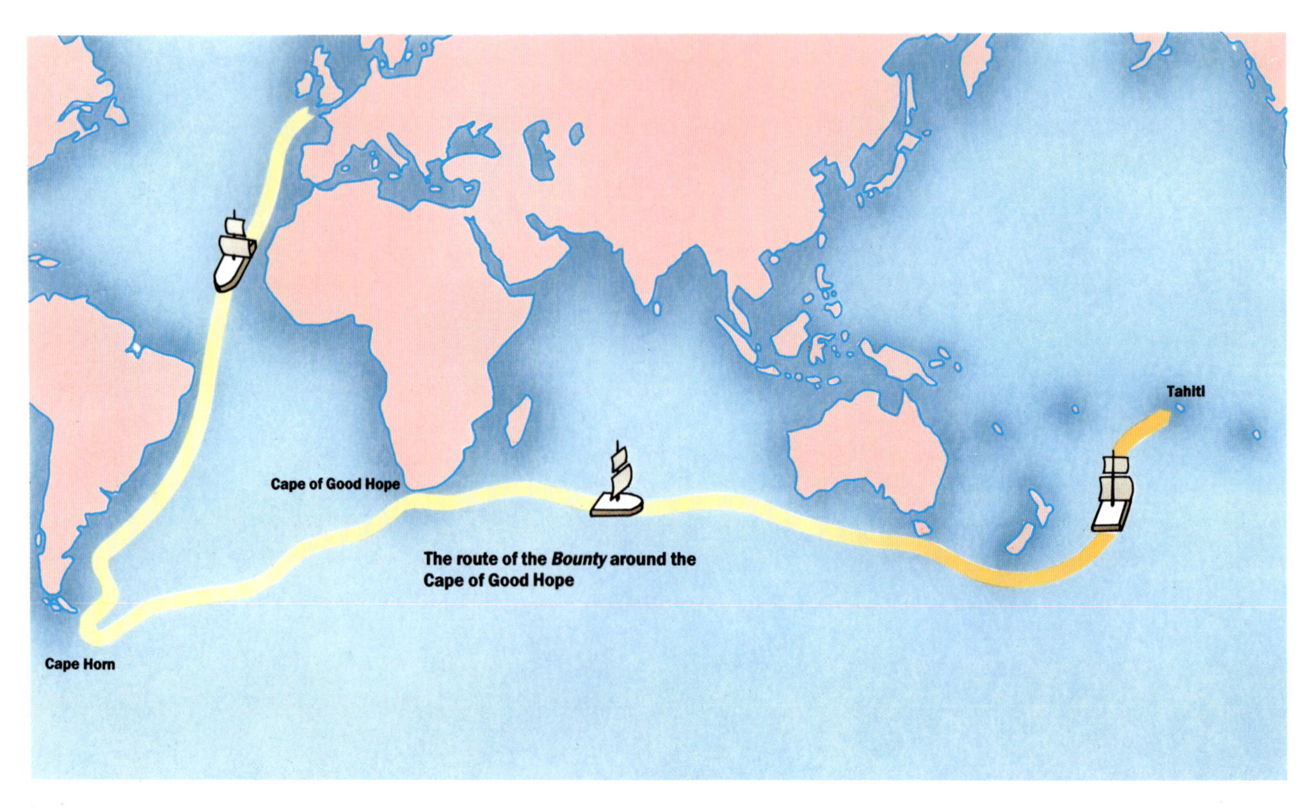

The *Bounty* met wintry storms off Cape Horn and battled against raging seas for weeks without making any progress.

Paradise Island

AT sunrise, the *Bounty's* crew crowded onto the deck to catch their first view of the island. Carefully, the ship was brought through the reefs and towards the shore. Then the morning mists cleared to reveal a wonderful landscape of steep rocks, deep valleys and waterfalls. It was richly covered with fruit trees and brightly coloured flowers. It seemed like an earthly paradise.

The crew were eager to go on shore after so many tedious months at sea. But before Bligh would allow them to leave, he made them promise not to tell the local people the real reason for their visit. Breadfruit was plentiful on the island, but the inhabitants must not think that Bligh meant to steal one of their most important food crops.

Soon, hundreds of canoes, large and small, paddled out from the shore. Within minutes, so many Tahitians had clambered onto the decks and **rigging** of the *Bounty* that Bligh could hardly find his own crew. But the islanders were friendly and welcoming. The Europeans brought them many things that they could not make on their island, especially metal tools. They were also proud to have the sailors as their guests, because it made them look important in the eyes of neighbouring islanders. Bligh realised this, and cleverly used the information to help him get the breadfruit trees he so desperately wanted. One day, when he was talking to one of the Tahitian chiefs, called Tinah, Bligh mentioned that he was thinking of going to visit other islands as well. Tinah didn't want him to leave.

'Here,' he said, 'you shall be plentifully supplied with everything you want. All here are your friends, and friends of King George: if you go to the other islands, you will have everything stolen from you.'

Bligh reminded Tinah that King George had sent him several presents, and asked him whether he was planning to send the King anything in return. 'Yes,' replied Tinah, 'I will send him anything I have.' He began to list things of value on the island: pigs, canoes, coconuts and breadfruit.

'Ah, breadfruit!' interrupted Bligh. 'Breadfruit trees are what King George would like.'

Tinah was delighted to find that King George was so easily pleased. Breadfruit trees grew all over the island, and he promised Bligh as many plants as he needed. The very next day, Bligh's men set up a nursery garden, and started to transplant young saplings into pots. It was easy work, because the local people were eager to help. Fletcher Christian and a party of crewmen were sent to set up a camp on shore to watch over the plants but, released from the routine of the *Bounty*, the crew led an easy life. They lazed on the beach, ate delicious food and were entertained by the friendly Tahitian girls.

The *Bounty* arrives at Tahiti and islanders row out to meet the ship. To the *Bounty's* crew, the island seemed like paradise after the long months at sea.

Tahiti

ALL this time, Bligh was studying Tahitian life. He visited chiefs and attended ceremonies, as they expected him to do. Tahiti was divided into a number of little kingdoms, each with its own chief who was chosen from one of the ruling families of the district. Wars were common between the kingdoms, so each chief had a group of warriors who fought their battles. But in peacetime the men and women of the warrior class lived a life of idleness and pleasure.

The ruling families of Tahiti were all related to each other, and were not allowed to marry with the common people, who were mostly farmers and labourers.

The Tahitians had plenty of food. Yams, bananas and breadfruit grew easily in the rich soil and warm wet climate. The children learnt from their parents how to look after the pigs and chickens and care for the plants. Girls helped their mothers make fine white cloth by beating the bark of the mulberry trees, and boys were expected to know how to build wooden boats and houses.

Before they grew up, both boys and girls had their bodies tattooed.

▷ A human sacrifice at a religious ceremony on Tahiti, performed in honour of the god Oro.

A painting of Oaitepaha Bay, Tahiti, by William Hodges, one of the artists who sailed to the Pacific with Captain Cook.

A Tahitian dancing girl, drawn by John Webber. The costumes of young women were made from bark which was beaten until it was soft.

Small black marks were cut into their skins using the sharp teeth of a bone or shell tool. First the tattooist dipped the teeth into a black liquid. Then he struck the tool several times with a stick, driving the points deep into the skin. The children often cried out with pain at each stroke, and the marks were sore for several days afterwards. But the Tahitians thought that the lines and patterns of the tattooes were very beautiful. They even persuaded Fletcher Christian and some of the other sailors to have themselves decorated.

By the end of the year, the crew of the *Bounty* became so used to life on Tahiti that Bligh found it difficult to maintain discipline. But he knew he could not leave for home until the breadfruit trees were firmly rooted in their pots. When Cook had visited Tahiti, he kept his men busy by taking his ship away every few weeks to survey other islands. Bligh could not do this. He had to keep the *Bounty* at the island to protect the men on shore from attacks by rival chiefs.

Bligh soon had proof that the crew had become careless and disobedient. On 25 December, when the *Bounty* was moved to a safer anchorage, the ship ran aground and had to be refloated. Then, on 5 January, three men deserted in the small cutter, stealing the boat when the mate of the watch was asleep. Bligh wrote angrily in his **logbook**, 'Such neglectful and worthless petty officers I believe never was in a ship like this'. The deserters were retaken with the help of the islanders and flogged.

The *Bounty* did not leave Tahiti until 4 April. The crew had been on 'Paradise Island' for five months, and many regretted leaving.

A Villainous Act

BLIGH was glad to set sail from Tahiti with his cargo of breadfruit trees. But some of his crew were unwilling to settle down again to the discipline of life aboard ship. Bligh's continual nagging and fault finding incensed them. Tension mounted and everyone was on edge.

Then, one fateful evening, Bligh accused Christian and several crew members of stealing coconuts from his store. Because no one would own up, he stopped everybody's daily tot of grog, and cut down the food rations. In the crew's eyes this was going too far. Christian was especially angry with Bligh. When he was invited to dine with the captain that night he refused. In desperation, he decided to escape on a raft to the nearest island. 'When you go, Christian, **the people** are ripe for anything,' whispered one of the crew. Christian thought hard. If the man was right, and the crew would support him, why didn't he start a mutiny? Within minutes his mind was made up. Quickly he persuaded three others to join him, then arming themselves with muskets from the ship's chest, they

The mutineers turning Bligh adrift. Some are preparing to fire on the helpless men in the launch.

went in search of Captain Bligh.

Bligh was taken completely by surprise. Without weapons, he was powerless to resist. The mutineers dragged him from his bed and forced him, half dressed, up onto the deck. He was held there for several hours while the mutineers decided what to do with him. Not all the sailors supported Christian, but, for the moment, they were powerless to help their captain. Christian decided that the best thing would be for Bligh to be **cast adrift**. He ordered the **jolly-boat** to be lowered, but it was worm-eaten, and began to sink. Even Christian didn't want to see Bligh drown, so he ordered the cutter to be launched.

When the sailors saw the larger boat being prepared, many decided to join Bligh. They pleaded with Christian to let them have the launch, the biggest of the *Bounty's* three boats. At first Christian refused: he knew that if he let nearly half the crew go, he would have barely enough men to sail her. 'You cannot turn us adrift in the cutter, Mr Christian,' said Purcell, the carpenter. 'Let us have the launch and not make a sacrifice of us.' At last, Christian agreed. The men who had decided to go with Bligh rushed to collect a few belongings and supplies from below. One by one they climbed onto the gangway. Christian realised that all the skilled men were leaving, so he forced Coleman, the armourer, and McIntosh and Norman, the carpenter's mates, to stay behind. Seeing their distress, Bligh shouted, 'Never fear, my lads, you can't all go with me, but I'll do you justice if ever I reach England.'

Bligh felt muskets being pressed into his back. 'Come, Captain Bligh,' said Christian. 'Your officers and men are now in the boat, and you must go with them. If you attempt to make the least resistance you will be instantly put to death.' Bligh knew that he had no choice but to obey. But before he stepped onto the gangway to the boat, he turned to face Christian. 'Is this a proper return for the many instances you have received my friendship?' he asked. 'That – Captain Bligh – that is the thing – I am in hell – I am in hell.'

The Open Boat

BLIGH walked with dignity down the gangway, and took his place in the launch. He looked around at the men who had decided to come with him. There was Nelson the gardener, Ledward the acting surgeon, and old Lebogue, the sail-maker. All were good men, loyal to their captain. Others in the boat, like Fryer the ship's master, and Purcell the carpenter, were troublemakers – or so Bligh thought. Fryer was mean and argumentative. He was only in the launch because Christian had not wanted him aboard the mutineers' ship.

Bligh counted 19 men in the boat, including himself. He knew that they would probably die, from starvation or drowning; or at best be stranded for years on some nearby island. All they had to eat and drink were 68 kilograms of ship's biscuit, 127 litres of water, six bottles of wine, seven litres of rum and a few pieces of pork. But at least they had some essential equipment – oars, sails, twine, fishing lines, hammocks, rope, canvas and some bags and boxes of clothes. The mutineers had allowed Bligh to keep his compass, his **quadrant**, his journals and the *Bounty's* logbook. To everyone's surprise, Christian sent Bligh his own sextant and navigational tables. But the mutineers would not give Bligh any muskets. He had to make do with just four **cutlasses**. His men rowed quickly away from the ship. Above the jeers and laughter of the mutineers, Bligh was sure he heard the cry 'Huzza for Tahiti!'

They decided to sail to Tofua, a small island about 30 miles away. Bligh asked himself whether he could possibly be to blame for the mutiny. No, he decided, it was no fault of his. Rather, he believed,

At Tofua, it seemed certain that the chasing canoes would capture Bligh's launch. Then Bligh ordered his men to throw their spare clothes into the water. The Tofuans stopped their canoes to gather them up. This allowed Bligh and his crew to escape from the island.

The route of open boat during its voyage to Timor.

Christian and other ungrateful villains must have seized the ship so that they could go back to their friends in Tahiti.

As the launch drew near to Tofua, Bligh and his men could see plumes of black smoke rising menacingly from the volcano at its centre. At first they found little to eat on the island; just a few coconuts and plantains and a dribble of water. Then some people appeared. They seemed welcoming, but a few days later, Bligh and his men heard a terrible sound. A large crowd of islanders was standing on the beach, clashing stones together with their hands. They looked warlike, and Bligh felt certain his men would be attacked. He ordered everyone back to the launch at once.

Soon Bligh was the only European left on the beach. Taking one of the local chiefs by the arm, he calmly walked down to the water's edge. Everyone – islanders and Bligh's men – watched in horrified silence. What would happen next? Bligh waded steadily out to the launch. Then the attack began. Stones flew through the air, and the islanders rushed to their canoes. One of Bligh's men, John Norton, was killed, but the rest got away with only a few bruises. It was a lucky escape.

Norton's death terrified everyone. Where could they go now? If they landed on another island, perhaps they would also be killed. Then Peckover, the gunner, remembered that there was a European settlement at Timor in the East Indies. But Timor was 3,600 miles away, and they did not have a chart. Worse still, they only had a few days' rations left.

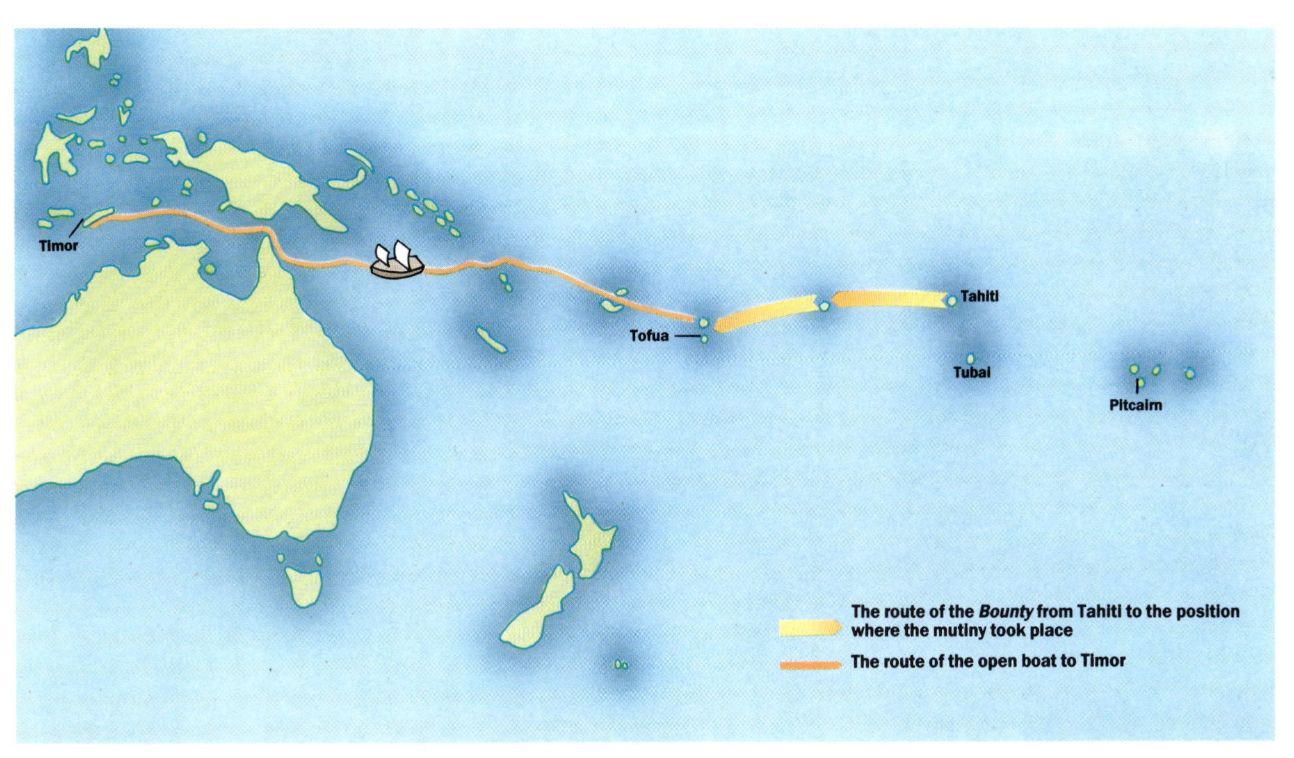

The Terrible Ordeal

'WELL, my lads,' said Bligh, 'are you all agreeable to live on two ounces of bread and a **gill** of water a day?' They thought longingly of friendly faces at Timor, and a safe passage home in a Dutch merchant ship. 'Yes sir,' replied each man in turn. And so began one of the greatest open boat voyages in the history of seafaring.

The next morning they saw the sun rise fiery red, a sure sign of bad weather. Within hours they ran into a storm, and huge waves filled the boat with water. Miraculously, they stayed afloat. A few days later they reached the Fiji Islands. The men could see streams of fresh water tumbling down the mountains, and bananas, plantains and yams growing in abundance. They gazed at them with longing, but did not dare to land, and sailed on without stopping.

Bligh's courage and leadership was an inspiration to everyone in the boat. He usually sat in the **stern**, making careful notes of the course they were steering. Sometimes he was so wet that he could hardly write, but still he managed to record many islands never before seen by Europeans. In the evenings, he led the men in prayers and songs to raise their spirits.

Every day, at dawn, noon and dusk, Bligh handed out the men's rations. To make sure that the provisions were fairly divided, he made some scales out of two coconut shells. Before each meal, he placed a pistol **shot** weighing 18 grams on one side of the scales to measure

The cup, scales and bullet weights used by Bligh to measure rations during the open boat voyage.

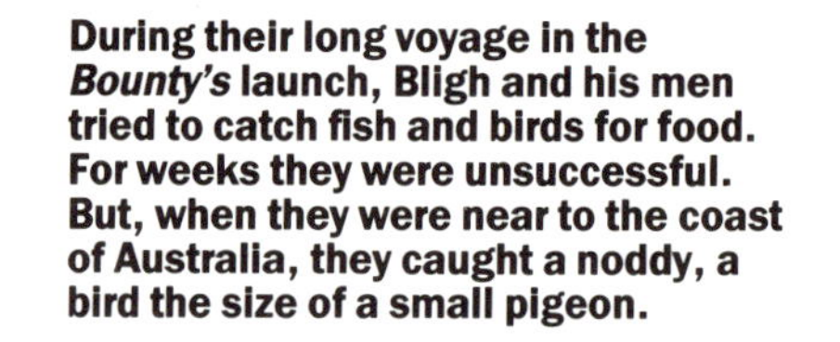

During their long voyage in the *Bounty's* launch, Bligh and his men tried to catch fish and birds for food. For weeks they were unsuccessful. But, when they were near to the coast of Australia, they caught a noddy, a bird the size of a small pigeon.

The astonished inhabitants of the Dutch colony at Timor meet Bligh and his men as they stagger ashore at the end of the open boat voyage. In real life, the Englishmen were thinner and much closer to death than the artist has shown.

each man's allowance of bread. Two weeks of rain chilled their cramped bodies but at least it gave them fresh water. Then one of the men caught a sea bird and killed it. Bligh carefully divided it, flesh, bone, guts, feet and beak, into 18 equal parts. They shared it amongst themselves as equally as possible.

On 29 May, 31 days after leaving the *Bounty*, they landed on an uninhabited island off the north-east coast of Australia. They made a fire by passing the rays of the sun through a magnifying glass, and cooked an oyster stew. The bird and the oysters were their first fresh food for weeks, and probably saved their lives. Now they were on dry land, some of the men began to argue with Bligh. 'If I had not brought you here, you would all have perished,' shouted Bligh in exasperation. 'Yes, sir,' replied Purcell sarcastically, 'if it had not been for you we should not have been here!'

But these quarrels ended once they set off again, and began the worst stage of their journey, from Australia to Timor. Their food and water had almost run out, and Bligh could see that his men were close to death. He recorded that they all had ghastly sunken faces, swollen legs, and skin covered with painful sores. After a week, they sighted Timor, and two days later, on 12 June, their boat sailed into harbour at the Dutch settlement. With tears of joy, Bligh and his men stumbled out of the boat and staggered along the beach. They were little more than walking skeletons, but they had survived!

The Mutineers

The *Bounty* in flames at Pitcairn. The timbers of the wooden ship burned long into the night, watched from the shore by the mutineers and their companions.

IN the hours after the mutiny, Fletcher Christian began to realise that he and the other mutineers were outcasts. If by some miracle Bligh got back to England, the navy was certain to send ships to the Pacific to hunt them down. Even if Bligh was lost without trace, Christian and the other mutineers could never return home to their friends and families. They would never be able to explain the loss of their captain and so many men. The mutineers would have to spend the rest of their lives in hiding. Christian knew that he was a doomed man, and the *Bounty* a doomed ship.

Things might have been better if the men on the *Bounty* had agreed a plan of how they would spend their lives together. But they all had different ideas. Some of the sailors were happy to laze around doing nothing, so long as there was plenty of rum and beautiful Tahitian women to entertain them. Others began to wish they had never joined in the mutiny, and pined for England and their homes and families. Some men had been kept on board against their will, because Christian thought that their skills would be useful, or because there was no more room in Bligh's launch.

Whatever their feelings, the mutineers had to find somewhere to live. They chose Christian as their new commander and, after consulting his charts, he decided they should settle on the island of Tubai, about 450 miles from Tahiti. But first the mutineers went to Tahiti to collect a large stock of pigs, goats and chickens. They also took Tahitian women to be their wives, and a group of Tahitian men as servants. In August 1789, they sailed to Tubai to live. But their plan went badly wrong. The people of the island were hostile to the settlers, and attacked them. After a few weeks, Christian was

forced to return with the *Bounty* to Tahiti. But before they left, the mutineers killed over 50 Tubaian men and women in revenge for their unfriendliness. It was a stupid and brutal act.

By now, the mutineers were feeling frightened and desperate. Most of the men decided that they would prefer to stay on Tahiti, and run the risk of being captured by the navy, rather than go on any more disastrous voyages. Christian did not agree. He, and eight others, voted to leave Tahiti again, and search for a remote, uninhabited island, where they could spend the rest of their lives undisturbed by passing ships, or by battles with local people. And so, early one morning, Christian gave orders for the *Bounty* secretly to set sail. There were just eight mutineers on board, together with a group of Tahitian men and women and two Tubaians. The remaining mutineers were left behind on Tahiti. They had no idea where the ship was going. The *Bounty's* fate remained a mystery for nearly 20 years.

For weeks, the *Bounty* sailed hopelessly from island to island. Nowhere seemed suitable. Then Christian noticed a description of a tiny island, called Pitcairn, in one of his books. It lay in a remote corner of the Pacific, and seemed the perfect choice.

After long weeks of searching, Christian and his crew finally found Pitcairn. It was uninhabited, with fertile land and fresh water. Within a few days, the men and women had taken everything they possessed from the *Bounty*. Then they had to decide whether or not to save the ship. The decision was made for them by Mat Quintal. While the others were still talking, he crept below decks and set fire to the vessel.

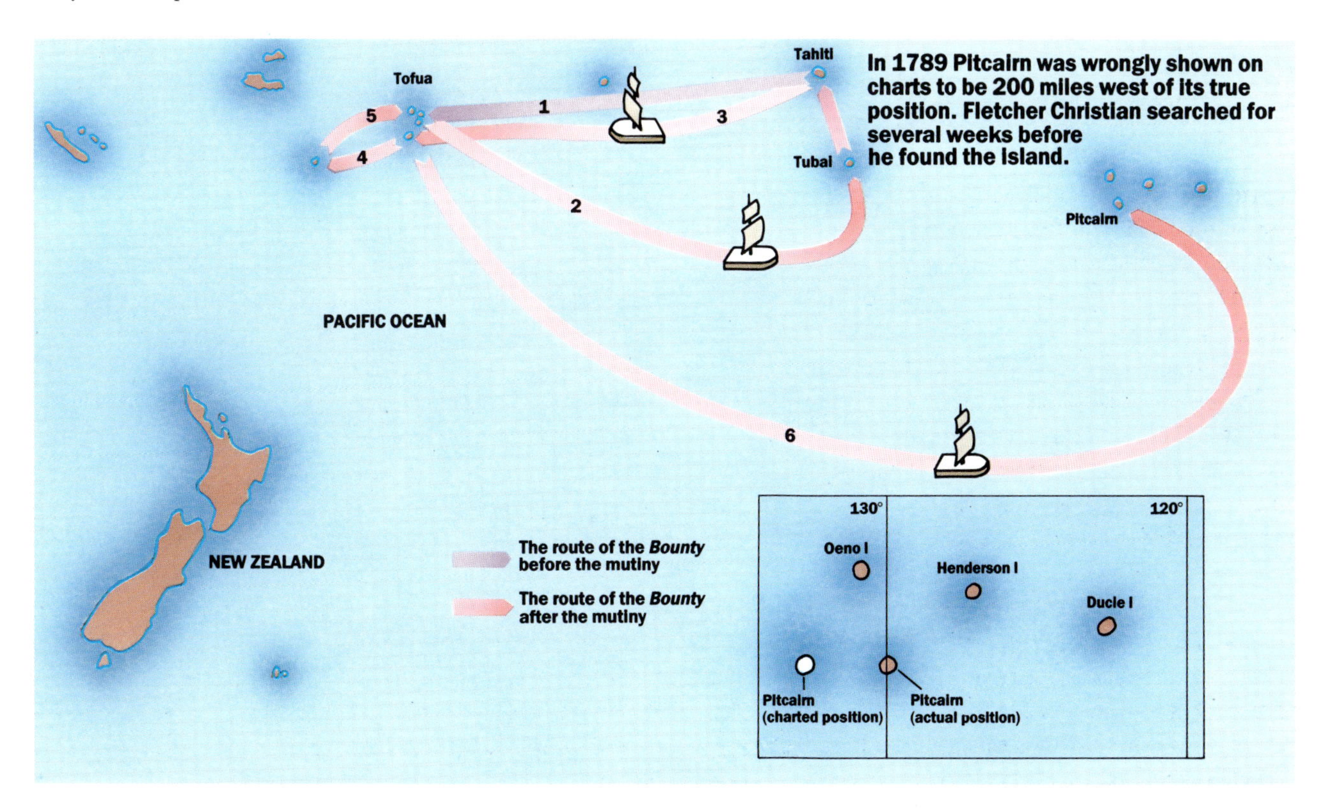

In 1789 Pitcairn was wrongly shown on charts to be 200 miles west of its true position. Fletcher Christian searched for several weeks before he found the island.

Pitcairn

THE settlers watched the *Bounty* burning late into the night. The women from Tahiti knew that the destruction of the ship ended any hope that they would see their homes and families again. When dawn came, they turned to face their new lives, alone on a tiny rocky island, a speck on the vast ocean.

The mutineers and their servants had everything they needed to survive. The soil of Pitcairn was rich and fertile, and the climate was warm. The steep hillsides were covered with lush forests, and the seas all around teemed with fish and lobsters. There were mulberry trees, mangoes, yams and breadfruit. But the island did not have any metal, which was essential if the settlers were to live in some comfort. Luckily, all the equipment on the ship had been saved. The men and women carried the *Bounty's* forge and cooking utensils up the steep slope, together with the timbers, rope, nails, tools and weapons. Now they understood why the people of the islands valued them so highly. It was tiring work, and took many weeks.

The men cleared some flat land high above the sea shore. There they built their homes, behind a screen of trees, using some timbers from the *Bounty* and logs felled on the island. The houses were half-English and half-Tahitian in design, with a living area on the ground floor, and a sleeping area above reached by a ladder.

There were twenty-eight people on Pitcairn: nine mutineers, twelve women, four men from Tahiti and two men from Tubai. They all had to get on peacably within a very small space – Pitcairn was only two miles long and one mile wide. There were many small communities on islands like this, leading happy lives. What kind of community would the mutineers build? The success of the Pitcairn settlement was entirely in their hands. They could not blame anyone else if it did not work.

But from the beginning, Christian and the other mutineers did not treat the Tahitians and Tubaians as equals. The men were forced to act as servants and labourers. The women, willingly or not, were divided among the men so that the mutineers had a wife each, while the Tahitian and Tubaian men shared one wife between two. The land on Pitcairn was also divided up unfairly; it was marked out into nine plots, one for each mutineer, but none for the islanders. At first, everybody accepted this system, but how long could such unjust arrangements last?

Soon after arriving at the island the settlers made a very disturbing discovery. They found pieces of carved timber, stone axes, pathways and the remains of old buildings. So they were not the first people to try to live on Pitcairn. The earlier settlers had been **Polynesians**, who were great navigators and explorers, and who made many voyages all over the Pacific Ocean. But what had happened to these people? Had they died or had they sailed away? The question must have made the island seem even more lonely to the mutineers.

The first settlers on Pitcairn lived on a small flat area of land at the top of a cliff. They built their homes behind a screen of trees so that they would not be seen by passing ships.

Breadfruit Bligh

BLIGH eventually returned to England on 14 March 1790. He was immediately **court-martialled** for losing his ship, but, since the Admiralty knew that it had been taken forcibly from him, Bligh was not held to blame. Later that year, he published a best-selling account of his voyage and the mutiny. Once the story of his nightmare journey to Timor became known, Bligh was treated like a celebrity. He was nicknamed 'Breadfruit Bligh', and praised for his courage, skill and determination. Scenes from the mutiny were even acted on the stage. One theatre advertised a show called 'The Pirates, or The Calamities of Capt. Bligh'; the entertainment included 'The Seizure of the Cabin of the *Bounty* by the Pirates' and a Tahitian dance.

Meanwhile, Captain Edward Edwards had been ordered to go to the Pacific and bring back the mutineers for trial. He left in HMS *Pandora* in August 1789. Edwards himself had been the victim of a mutiny, in 1782, and he was well-known for his strict discipline.

ROYALTY-THEATRE,
Well-Street, near Goodman's-Fields.

This prefent THURSDAY, May 6, 1790,
WILL BE PRESENTED
A NEW MUSICAL PIECE, called
TAR againſt PERFUME:
Or, The SAILOR PREFERRED.
Coxſwain, Mr. MATHEWS. William, Mr. BIRKETT. Old Slop, Mr. REES.
And Monſieur Le Friz, (the Perfumer,) Mr. WEWITZER.
Suſan, Miſs WILLIAMS.
A NEW DANCE, compoſed by Mr. BOURKE, called
THE MERRY BLOCK-MAKERS.
By Monf. FERRERE, Mad. FOUZZI, Mad FERRERE, Mr. JEANI, Mr. BOURKE, &c.
A MUSICAL ENTERTAINMENT, called
A PILL FOR THE DOCTOR:
Or, The TRIPLE WEDDING.
Sailor, Mr. BIRKETT. Dr. Lotion, Mr. REES. Farmer, Mr. MATHEWS.
And Peſtle, the Doctor's Man, Mr. WEWITZER.
Polly, Miſs WILLIAMS Dorothy, Mrs. SAUNDERS.
Lydia, Miſs E. WILLIAMS. And Goody, Mrs. BURNETT.
To conclude with a DANCE by the Characters.
A FAVOURITE SONG, by Miſs DANIEL.
The Whole to conclude with (the 4th Time) A FACT, TOLD IN ACTION, called
The PIRATES:
OR,
The Calamities of Capt. BLIGH.
Exhibiting a full Account of his Voyage, from his taking Leave at the Admiralty.
AND SHEWING,
The BOUNTY falling down the River THAMES.
The Captain's Reception at OTAHEITE, and exchanging the *Britiſh Manufactures* for the BREAD-FRUIT TREES. With an OTAHEITEAN DANCE.
The Attachment of the OTAHEITEAN WOMEN to, and then Diſtreſs at parting from, the BRITISH SAILORS.
An exact Repreſentation of
The SEISURE of Capt. BLIGH, in the Cabin of the BOUNTY, by the Pirates.
With the affecting Scene of forcing the Captain and his faithful Followers into the Boat.
Their Diſtreſs at Sea, and Repulſe by the Natives of One of the *Friendly Iſlands*.
Their miraculous Arrival at the *Cape of Good Hope*, and their friendly Reception by the Governor.
DANCES and CEREMONIES of the HOTTENTOTS
On their Departure. And their happy Arrival in England.
Rehearſed under the immediate Inſtruction of a Perſon who was on-board the Bounty, Store-Ship.
*** The Doors to be opened at Half paſt Five and to begin at Half paſt Six o'Clock preciſely.
BOXES, 3s. 6d.—PIT, 2s. 6d.—FIRST GALLERY, 1s. 6d.—UPPER GALLERY, 1s.
Nothing under full Price will be taken nor any Money returned:
Places for the Boxes may be taken at the Stage-Door from Ten till Three o'Clock every Day.
VIVANT REX & REGINA.
BOOKS of the PILL for the DOCTOR to be had at the Theatre; and, to prevent Impoſition, the Proprietors have ordered that no more ſhall be taken for them than SIX-PENCE each.

A playbill advertising a performance of a play about the mutiny at the Royalty Theatre, London. Events like this helped to make Bligh a celebrity.

The *Providence* was a brand new merchant ship, larger than the *Bounty* and more suitable for an expedition to Tahiti.

A 19th-century cartoon showing Bligh at the mercy of the mutineers. The artist presents Bligh as the victim and the mutineers as violent and cruel.

Though Bligh had lost his ship to the mutineers, he had not lost the confidence of Sir Joseph Banks or the Admiralty, his principal backers. Banks presented Bligh to King George III. Shortly afterwards, the Admiralty promoted Bligh from lieutenant to **commander** and then to **post-captain**. In 1791 he was appointed captain of HMS *Providence*, and given orders to undertake a second breadfruit expedition. This journey went much more smoothly. The Admiralty officials had learned from Bligh's experience with the *Bounty* and allowed him to take a larger ship and to select a much more reliable crew.

In April 1792, Bligh arrived once more at Tahiti. On this visit, he noticed that many changes had taken place during the three years he had been away. The Tahitians were still friendly and hospitable, but, instead of their local clothes (light and suitable for a hot climate) they were proudly wearing filthy old shirts, waistcoats and trousers that the sailors had given them. Even more worrying, local skills were in decline. As the Tahitians explained, there was no point in making cloth or stone axes laboriously by hand when these things could be bought from passing ships in exchange for a few pigs or fresh vegetables. Worst of all, the Tahitians had also exchanged local produce for guns, which made wars among the islanders far more dangerous and deadly. Bligh was shocked and saddened to see how much damage had been caused on the island by contact with Europeans.

There was little Bligh could do to persuade the Tahitian people to return to their old ways, and so he concentrated on collecting his cargo of 2,126 breadfruit trees. He made a speedy journey across to the West Indies, and then back home to England. The second breadfruit voyage had been uneventful – and a complete success!

The Wreck

THE *Pandora* arrived at Tahiti in March 1791. Three of the *Bounty's* crew gave themselves up immediately. They were legally innocent of mutiny – they had been below decks when Christian seized control of the ship. But Captain Edwards immediately ordered them to be clapped in irons. The mutineers on the island were betrayed by a sailor from a ship that had recently anchored at Tahiti. One night, he led Edwards' men to a Tahitian hut. Quietly, they felt the feet of the sleeping bodies. The mutineers were all used to wearing shoes, and Edwards' men easily identified them. They arrested the mutineers and took them back to the ship.

Edwards sailed from Tahiti in May, and went in search of the *Bounty*. Conditions on board ship were grim for the captive mutineers. Edwards had arranged for a special cage to be built to hold them. Fourteen men were crammed into a space measuring 3.35m by 5.49m. It had two small air holes at the side, and another in the roof, secured by a bolt. Inside, the mutineers were forced to lie naked, chained hand and foot. When it rained, the cell leaked; when the sun shone it was like an oven.

The mutineers' sweat ran in streams down to the **scuppers** and attracted flies and maggots.

Edwards failed to find the *Bounty*. Soon, he turned for home. He was not a skilled navigator and, on 28 August, the *Pandora* struck the Great Barrier Reef off the northern Australian coast. In minutes, she was leaking badly. The crew rushed to man the pumps, but their efforts could not stop the water rising. Eventually, the *Pandora* was driven over the reef into the calm lagoon beyond. But all attempts to repair her failed, and then the pumps broke down. The ship was doomed . . .

Locked in their cell, the mutineers were terrified. They feared they would be left to drown like rats. They managed to break out of their chains, but Edwards ordered new ones to be fitted. At dawn, Edwards gave orders for all men to abandon ship, and then, at last, ordered the mutineers' release. The armourer's mate hurried to unfasten the prisoners' chains but in a panic, one mutineer jumped overboard, still wearing his irons, and was drowned at once. Then the master-at-arms, who had not heard Edwards' final order, closed the escape hatch. The mutineers inside thought they were doomed. But a brave sailor clambered up her broken **hull** to open the cell, and finally, with cries of joy, the mutineers were free.

Later that morning, the bedraggled survivors gathered on a nearby sandbank. Out of 134 on board, 35 had died, including 4 mutineers. They were, they calculated, 1,100 miles away from the nearest European settlement. Like Bligh and his men, they suffered terribly, but eventually they made the dangerous crossing by open boat to Timor.

The *Pandora* is wrecked on the Great Barrier Reef. The crew and some prisoners escape in the ship's boats.

Court Martial

THE mutineers who had survived the wreck of the *Pandora* were brought to England for trial in September 1792. Bligh was not present – he was away on his second breadfruit voyage – but he had left descriptions of what had happened during the mutiny, to be used as evidence against the mutineers.

The mutineers were kept on board the prison ship *Hector*, anchored in Portsmouth. They knew that mutiny was a terrible crime. The law said that any sailor who had not tried to defend Bligh was just as guilty as Christian and the others who had planned the mutiny. Most of the prisoners knew that they had little hope of escaping execution.

One of the men on trial was Peter Heywood, a midshipman on the *Bounty*. One witness said that he had seen Heywood with a cutlass in his hand, another that Heywood had laughed in Bligh's face, then walked away. No one had seen Heywood try to help Bligh or try to get into the boat with him. Bligh himself was adamant that Heywood was one of the leading mutineers. 'His baseness is beyond description' he wrote to Heywood's mother.

Heywood's only defence was his youth; he was just 17 at the time of the mutiny. He admitted that Bligh had always treated him very kindly.

The evidence seemed damning, and should have convicted him. But Heywood had many important friends and relatives in the navy who were determined to save his life. One of the judges was Captain Bertie, a relative of his; another judge was a

A portrait of the mutineer Peter Heywood.

Peter Heywood on trial for mutiny before Admiral Lord Hood and twelve post-captains in the great cabin of HMS *Duke*.

close friend of the Heywood family. Heywood was found guilty, but the court recommended that he should be pardoned.

The other men on trial were ordinary sailors with no influential friends. Some had a genuine defence; Coleman, McIntosh and Norman tried to get into the launch with Bligh, but had been ordered back aboard the *Bounty* because it was already full. The court pardoned them and set them free. Byrne, the ship's blind musician had also tried to leave with Bligh, but had been left behind in the cutter. Morrison claimed that the only reason why he had not got into the launch was because it was already full of men. Musprat said that he had picked up a gun only to help recapture the ship. All three escaped hanging. Others were not so lucky. Ellison, Burkitt and Millward had all been seen carrying weapons; two had even acted as Christian's sentries. They came from poor families, and had no friends among the court. They were hanged.

Bligh's good reputation was damaged by the court martial. Thanks to the efforts of the Heywood family many people in England now believed that Bligh's violent temper and his threats against his men were the cause of the mutiny. Peter Heywood was more fortunate. After he was freed, he was offered a place on Lord Hood's flagship and was promoted. In Portsmouth, the ordinary people said that money bought Heywood's life, but that Ellison, Burkitt and Millward 'fell sacrifice to their poverty'

Murder on Pitcairn

In October 1790, the Tahitian wife of Jack Williams, one of the mutineers, fell down a steep cliff on Pitcairn while collecting birds' eggs for food. Her tragic death sparked off a series of murderous, bloody feuds, which lasted for almost ten years and left many men dead. It is hard to discover exactly what happened during this dark period in Pitcairn's history, because the settlers left no written records. Most of the story that follows is based on island traditions passed down by word of mouth, and written down many years later.

The old stories record that Jack Williams was very lonely after his wife's death. Eventually, he went to ask Christian and the other mutineers to help him steal one of the three women who were shared by the islanders. Reluctantly, Christian agreed.

This act shattered the fragile peace on Pitcairn. The island men, and some of the women, now hated the white men. They could not escape – there was no ship – and so they plotted to kill the mutineers instead. Christian got to hear of this plan, and decided that the ringleaders must be executed. He ordered four of the islanders to kill the other two; they dared not refuse, but they waited for the chance to take their revenge.

A portrait of the mutineer Alexander Smith in old age. It was drawn on Pitcairn in 1825 by the captain of a visiting ship. Smith's real name was John Adams, but he changed his name when he signed on for the voyage.

The children of mutineers on Pitcairn Island. George Young, the son of Edward Young, with his wife Hannah Adams, the daughter of John Adams (Alexander Smith), and their child.

And so, one day in 1793, the Tahitian men met together in secret, picked up their guns and went into the fields where some of the mutineers were working. Within an hour Williams, Mills, Martin, Brown and, it is said, Fletcher Christian, lay dead on the ground around the village and in the fields nearby. The killings continued, and by 1800, there was only one man – Alexander Smith – left alive on the island. After taking part in several murders he decided to devote the rest of his life to religion. He became the leader of the little community on Pitcairn, and, under his guidance, the surviving women and children were able to lead lives that were at least free from violence and fear.

In 1808 an American ship, the *Topaz*, found Pitcairn by accident and stopped there for food and water. The captain and crew were amazed to discover Alexander Smith living on the island with a group of Tahitian women and children, most of them descendants of the dead mutineers. The mystery of the *Bounty* was solved at last.

One mystery remains, however. Did Fletcher Christian really die on Pitcairn, or did he escape from the island and find his way home? One day, in 1808 or 1809, Peter Heywood (who was by then a navy captain) was walking along the docks in Plymouth when he saw a man who looked just like Christian. The unknown man saw him, too, looked frightened and ran away before Heywood could catch him. At about the same time, there were rumours circulating in Cumberland (where Christian was born) that he had come back, and was visiting an old aunt there. Could Christian have been in hiding in England all those years? The evidence is very slight, and it is hard to believe that Christian could ever have reached England safely and secretly, even if he had escaped from Pitcairn. But it is just possible . . .

Man or Monster?

Bligh in later life, wearing a medal that was presented to him after the battle of Camperdown.

BLIGH'S second breadfruit voyage was a triumphant success. But if Bligh expected a hero's welcome when he returned to England in 1793, he was cruelly disappointed.

Two important events had taken place while Bligh was abroad. Firstly, the mutineers' trial had been held, in 1792. Although some of the mutineers had been found guilty and punished, the court had also heard many accusations against Bligh by lawyers seeking to defend them. Secondly, Edward Christian (Fletcher Christian's brother, and Professor of Law at Cambridge University) had organised another, unofficial, trial. He claimed this was an independent 'court of inquiry' into the cause of the mutiny. But his real aim was to defend his brother. Any evidence which created sympathy for Fletcher Christian was included and any which favoured Bligh was left out. Edward Christian's conclusion was that his brother was a decent man who had been driven by Bligh's tyranny to mutiny, in desperation and frenzy.

Sadly for Bligh, most people believed that Edward Christian's inquiry was an honest attempt to find the cause of the mutiny. The image it created of Bligh as a ranting bully is still widely accepted today.

However, the navy soon decided that it could not do without Bligh's skills as a captain. He went back to sea again in 1795 to join the English fleet in its war against France. And he played a leading part in two of the greatest sea battles of his day – the battles of Camperdown (1797) and Copenhagen (1801).

During his career, Bligh suffered two more mutinies, at the **Nore**

There have been several film versions of the *Bounty* story. Bligh is usually portrayed as a brutal officer, whose stubborn behaviour was the cause of the mutiny.

Bligh's ship, the *Director,* finishing off the Dutch flagship *Vrijheid* – meaning Liberty – during the battle of Camperdown. The carnage on the enemy ship was appalling, with 59 dead, and 98 wounded.

in 1797, and in Australia in 1808. At the Nore, the men of the fleet mutinied against their captains, demanding better pay and conditions. There is no evidence that they made any complaints about Bligh personally. The other mutiny, called the Rum Rebellion, took place in New South Wales in Australia. Before Bligh arrived there as governor general, the colony was run by a group of dishonest army officers and some wealthy sheep farmers. When Bligh tried to stop an illegal trade in rum organised by the soldiers, the army imprisoned him in his own house. Help eventually arrived from England, and he returned home to London, where he was promoted to the rank of vice-admiral. He died in 1817, aged 64.

Since his death, Bligh has become one of the best known of all English seamen. In most versions of the story of the mutiny on the *Bounty*, Bligh is shown as a brutal monster and Fletcher Christian as a dashing hero. This is unfair to Bligh. But it shows that Edward Christian's attacks two hundred years ago were very clever and effective.

In real life, Captain Bligh was a great navigator and explorer. But he had many faults. He often distrusted his junior officers, making favourites of some and criticising others unfairly.

Fletcher Christian, too, had his good qualities. He was an active and intelligent young man with a warm and attractive personality. But he desperately wanted to be liked by everyone, both officers and men. He could not carry the responsibilities that went with being an officer. And, when he became leader of the mutineers, he was guilty of the senseless murder of dozens of islanders at Tubai. This was something Bligh would never have done.

There were many mutinies in the eighteenth century, some of them far more important than the mutiny on the *Bounty*. Compared with the mutiny at the Nore, that great act of rebellion by English sailors, the mutiny led by Fletcher Christian was a trivial event caused by a petty quarrel. But it is the story of the *Bounty* which is still remembered today.

Key Dates

9 September 1754	William Bligh born in Portsmouth
20 March 1776	Bligh appointed master in HMS *Resolution* on Cook's Third Voyage
14 February 1779	Cook murdered by natives on Hawaii
4 February 1781	Bligh marries Elizabeth Betham
Summer 1785	Bligh takes command of Campbell's new ship the *Britannia*. Fletcher Christian joins the crew
5 August 1787	Bligh appointed commander of breadfruit voyage
23 December 1787	Bligh sets sail from Portsmouth
26 October 1788	Bligh arrives at Tahiti
4 April 1789	Bligh leaves Tahiti with breadfruit
28 April 1789	Mutiny on the *Bounty*
6 June 1789	Christian and *Bounty* arrive at Tahiti
14 June 1789	Bligh lands his launch at Timor
19 June 1789	Christian and *Bounty* sail from Tahiti for Tubai
20 September 1789	Christian and *Bounty* return to Tahiti and leave those who wish to settle there
21 January 1790	Christian and core of mutineers land at Pitcairn
14 March 1790	Bligh returns to England
10 August 1790	Captain Edwards appointed to command the *Pandora*
23 March 1791	*Pandora* arrives at Tahiti
8 May 1791	*Pandora* leaves Tahiti with captured mutineers
3 August 1791	Bligh departs in the *Providence* for second breadfruit voyage
29 August 1791	*Pandora* wrecked on Great Barrier Reef
18 June 1792	Surviving prisoners brought back to England
12 September 1792	Court martial of mutineers opens
29 October 1792	Three mutineers executed at Spithead
7 August 1793	Bligh returns from second breadfruit voyage
Autumn 1793	Christian and four other white men murdered on Pitcairn
Autumn 1793	Murder of surviving native men on Pitcairn
April-May 1797	Spithead and Nore Mutinies
11 October 1797	Battle of Camperdown
2 April 1801	Battle of Copenhagen
29 April 1805	Bligh appointed Governor of New South Wales
28 September 1808	Pitcairn colony discovered by Mayhew Folger of the *Topaz*
25 October 1810	Bligh returns to England from Australia
7 December 1817	Bligh dies

Fate of the *Bounty's* Crew

WILLIAM BLIGH [Lieutenant], aged 33, captain of the *Bounty*. He rose to the rank of Vice-Admiral of the Blue and died in 1817, aged 64.

JOHN FRYER [Master], aged 33. Forced to accompany Bligh in the launch. Later appointed master of the *Inconstant*.

WILLIAM COLE [Boatswain]. Joined Bligh in the launch. Returned safely to England.

WILLIAM PECKOVER [Gunner]. Joined Bligh in the launch. Returned safely to England.

WILLIAM PURCELL [Carpenter]. Forced to accompany Bligh in the launch. Disciplined on his return to England.

THOMAS HUGGAN [Surgeon]. Drank himself to death on the voyage to Tahiti.

THOMAS LEDWARD [Surgeon's Mate]. Joined Bligh in the launch. Disappeared, possibly drowned on the voyage from Batavia to England.

FLETCHER CHRISTIAN [Master's Mate], aged 22. Leader of the mutiny. Probably murdered on Pitcairn in 1793.

WILLIAM ELPHINSTONE [Master's Mate], aged 36. Joined Bligh in the launch but never recovered from the ordeal and died in Batavia.

JOHN HALLET [Midshipman], aged 15. Joined Bligh in the launch and returned safely to England. Died a lieutenant on board HMS *Penelope*.

THOMAS HAYWARD [Midshipman], aged 20. Drowned when in command of the *Swift*, a sloop of war, which sank in a typhoon in the China Sea.

PETER HEYWOOD [Midshipman], aged 15. Mutineer who stayed on the *Bounty*. Sentenced to death by court martial and subsequently pardoned. Reached the rank of post-captain before dying in 1831.

ROBERT TINKLER [Midshipman], aged 17. Joined Bligh in the launch. Later rose to be a post-captain.

EDWARD YOUNG [Midshipman], aged 21. Mutineer. Died on Pitcairn of lung disease in 1800.

GEORGE STEWART [Midshipman], aged 21. Stayed on the *Bounty*. Drowned in wreck of the *Pandora*.

PETER LINKLETTER [Quartermaster], aged 30. Joined Bligh in the launch but did not recover from the ordeal and died in Batavia.

JOHN NORTON [Quartermaster], aged 34. Joined Bligh in the launch but was murdered by natives on Tofua.

GEORGE SIMPSON [Quartermaster's Mate], aged 27. Joined Bligh in the launch and returned safely to England.

JAMES MORRISON [Boatswain's Mate], aged 27. Mutineer who stayed on *Bounty*. Sentenced to death by court martial and subsequently pardoned. Appointed gunner to HMS *Blenheim* and drowned when she sank in 1807.

JOHN MILLS [Gunner's Mate], aged 39. Mutineer. Shot by natives on Pitcairn in 1793.

CHARLES NORMAN [Carpenter's Mate], aged 24. Loyal to Bligh but forced to remain on *Bounty*. Acquitted at the court martial.

THOMAS McINTOSH [Carpenter's Mate], aged 25. Loyal to Bligh but forced to remain on *Bounty*. Acquitted at the court martial.

LAWRENCE LEBOGUE [Sailmaker], aged 40. Joined Bligh in the launch and returned safely to England.

JOSEPH COLEMAN [Armourer], aged 36. Loyal to Bligh but forced to remain on the *Bounty*. Acquitted at the court martial.

CHARLES CHURCHILL [Corporal], aged 28. Mutineer. Murdered by Thompson at Tahiti.

HENRY HILLBRANT [Cooper], aged 24. Mutineer. Drowned in the wreck of the *Pandora*.

WILLIAM MUSPRAT [Steward], aged 27. Mutineer. Sentenced to death by court martial but acquitted on a technicality in 1793.

JOHN SAMUEL [Clerk and Steward], aged 26. Joined Bligh in the launch. Later promoted to paymaster after his return to England.

THOMAS HALL [Ship's Cook], aged 38. Joined Bligh in the launch. Died at Batavia, 11 October 1793.

JOHN SMITH [Commander's Cook], aged 36. Joined Bligh in the launch. Returned safely to England.

ROBERT LAMB [Butcher], aged 21. Joined Bligh in the launch. Died on the return journey to England.

RICHARD SKINNER [Able Seaman], aged 22. Mutineer. Drowned in the wreck of the *Pandora*.

ALEXANDER SMITH [Able Seaman], aged 20. Mutineer. Died on Pitcairn in 1829.

THOMAS BURKITT [Able Seaman], aged 25. Mutineer. Sentenced to death and hanged in 1792.

JOHN MILLWARD [Able Seaman], aged 21. Mutineer. Sentenced to death and hanged in 1792.

JOHN WILLIAMS [Able Seaman], aged 26. Mutineer. Shot by natives on Pitcairn in 1793.

JOHN SUMNER [Able Seaman], aged 22. Mutineer. Drowned in the wreck of the *Pandora*.

MATTHEW THOMPSON [Able Seaman], aged 37. Mutineer. Murdered by islanders in Tahiti.

JAMES VALENTINE [Able Seaman], aged 28. Died on 9 October 1788 of blood poisoning on the way to Tahiti.

MICHAEL BYRNE [Able Seaman and Musician], aged 26. Loyal to Bligh but forced to remain on the *Bounty*. Acquitted at the court martial.

WILLIAM McCOY [Able Seaman], aged 23. Mutineer. Fell off a cliff on Pitcairn whilst drunk. He may have been pushed.

MATTHEW QUINTAL [Able Seaman], aged 21. Mutineer. Murdered by Young and Smith on Pitcairn in 1799.

ISAAC MARTIN [Able Seaman], aged 30. Mutineer. Shot by natives on Pitcairn in 1793.

THOMAS ELLISON [Able Seaman], aged 19. Mutineer. Sentenced to death and hanged in 1792.

DAVID NELSON [Gardener]. Joined Bligh in the launch. Died of a fever at Coupang, 18 July 1789.

WILLIAM BROWN [Gardener's Assistant], aged 25. Mutineer. Shot by natives on Pitcairn in 1793.

Glossary

Admiralty The government office responsible for the administration of the Royal Navy

Cast adrift To place people in the ship's boat and leave them to the mercy of wind and waves.

Chart A map for sailors showing coasts, rocks and other features in the sea.

Colony A country or area that is owned and controlled by another country.

Commander The naval rank immediately below that of post-captain; in command of a small ship.

Commissioned officer An officer appointed by the King, bearing the rank of lieutenant and above.

Compass A navigational instrument which sailors use to find the direction in which their ship is sailing. The needle on the compass will always point to the magnetic north.

Cutlass A short sword with a curved blade, used by seamen.

Deptford An important naval dockyard on the south bank of the River Thames.

Fix a position To find out the exact location of a ship at sea.

Gill A measure of liquid equal to 142 millilitres.

Hull The upper deck, sides, and bottom of a ship.

Jolly-boat A small ship's boat. The *Bounty* had three boats; this was the smallest.

Lash A whip made from nine lengths of cord (cat-o'-nine tails).

Logbook A daily record of the activities on board ship which was kept by the captain.

Marines Soldiers especially trained for fighting at sea.

Mile The unit of distance used at sea is the nautical mile. The standard nautical mile is 1,852 metres – slightly longer than the land mile, which is 1,609 metres.

Musket A long-barrelled gun fired from the shoulder.

Navigation The art of guiding a ship from one place to another safely and efficiently.

Nore A navy anchorage at the mouth of the River Thames, England.

Pay off At the end of a voyage the crew's wages were paid, and all the ship's expenses were settled.

The people The seamen on a warship who were neither commissioned nor warrant officers (*see page* 4).

Polynesians The people who live on several island groups in the South Pacific.

Post-captain The naval rank immediately above that of commander. A post-captain was in command of a ship large enough to be in one of the six divisions of the navy's warships.

Quadrant A navigational instrument used by the sailors to find out the ship's position north or south of the Equator.

Rigging Ropes which were used on the ships to support the masts and to raise and lower the sails.

Scuppers These were holes in the ship's side to let the water on deck drain away into the sea.

Seafaring Going to sea for a living.

Sextant A navigational instrument used by sailors to help work out a ship's position.

Shot A small iron ball fired from a gun.

South Seas The old term for the Pacific Ocean.

Stern The back of a ship.

Warrant officer An officer who was a specialist in his field e.g. boatswain, gunner, carpenter.

Watch A sailor's period of duty on ship, normally four hours in eight.

Index

PRINTED IN BELGIUM BY
proost
INTERNATIONAL BOOK PRODUCTION